A CHILDREN'S COLOR OF JAMESTOWN IN VIRGINIA

BY

PRISCILLA HUNT

ILLUSTRATED BY

F. RICHARD VRANIAN

THE DIETZ PRESS, RICHMOND, VIRGINIA

A LONG, long time ago, three sailing ships left a port at old England across the ocean. They were very small boats if you could see them beside the big ships of today, but they were beautiful as their large sails flapped with the breeze. These three little ships were named the Discovery, the Godspeed, and the Susan Constant. On the sailing ships were about one hundred Englishmen and a few boys. When the three boats left England, there may have been people waving their hands and telling them good-bye, because these men and boys were going far, far away to a new land.

The land to which the men and boys were sailing was called Virginia. It was a wilderness where Indians and wild animals lived, and few people knew much about it. But to the people in England, Virginia was thought to be a rich land. Englishmen thought they would find gold, beautiful rare stones, and furs. Some of the Englishmen coming over on the three little sailing ships wanted to get rich; others wanted to seek adventure; and some wanted to teach the Indians about Christ, and plant the Anglican Church, the church of England, in the New World.

They sailed on and on for hundreds and hundreds of miles over the blue water of the Atlantic Ocean. Sometimes storms came up and tossed the little ships up and down on the high waves. At other times the weather was clear and sunny and the deep sea was calm—so calm that there was hardly enough breeze to push against the sails and drive the three boats onward. Some nights were so dark that the men and boys couldn't see the other ships, but many nights were warm and lighted with a big bright moon. Always the Discovery, Godspeed and Susan Constant sailed westward—westward to the land of Virginia and to a new home for these brave Englishmen and English boys.

It took them about five months to sail across the wide ocean. During the beautiful month of May, they landed in Virginia and then came up a wide river which they named the James River in honor of the King of England. As they sailed up the James they reached a stretch of land where the water was deep enough to anchor their boats. This was just what they were looking for, so the sails were lowered and the three little ships heaved to shore. A few of the men climbed over the sides, down the rope ladders and waded in the water to the shore. They were thankful to again be on land and they named the spot of land Jamestown—also after their king.

The next morning was an exciting time. All of the men and boys left the ships and came ashore. Their minister, Robert Hunt, knelt on the ground and prayed to God. He thanked Him for having watched over them and for having brought them safely to Virginia and to Jamestown. Some time later, Mr. Hunt held church services under an old tent which the men had stretched across small trees. Logs were used for seats and a big trunk of a tree was used for the pulpit. All of the men and boys attended the services. It was the first English church in Virginia.

You must remember that the English colonists were not the only people in Virginia. Indians were there. Many of them. They had been in Virginia for years and years. Soon after the colonists landed, the Indians came to watch and see what was happening. They were dressed in animal skins and wore shells and beads for jewelry. Some wore colored feathers. The Englishmen had short hair and beards, so the Indians looked strange to the Englishmen and the Englishmen looked strange to the Indians. The Indians believed that all of the land in Virginia belonged to them, and were not certain what the Englishmen planned to do in Virginia.

It was not long before little unfriendly things made the Indians angry. They began to suspect the white strangers who had come to Virginia and their hunting grounds. They thought the Englishmen might take their homes and their great forests from them. One day no Indians came around to watch the men at Jamestown and as the men and boys worked in the fields and fort, they did not think anything was wrong. Suddenly a band of painted Indian warriors attacked the colonists with bows and arrows and killed a boy and wounded a few of the men.

This was a warning to the colonists. For weeks they worked long and hard in building a palisade for protection. The English not only feared the Indians, but also the Spanish. The palisade was like a tall, sharp-pointed fence in the shape of a triangle that the Indians couldn't climb over. Cannon from the ships were mounted on it. If anyone attacked, all of the colonists could get within this stockade and defend themselves by shooting out. It was a crude, old-fashioned kind of fort, but it was what the white men needed to keep from being killed. None of them would go in the fields again without carrying guns.

During the first weeks the men and boys, now called colonists, lived on the ships. When they stayed on land at night they lived in tents and under the trees. The weather was warm at this time of year in Virginia, and deer flies swarmed around the settlers. Every day some of them worked, building huts to live in, a church, a storehouse to keep food and other goods, all within the fort. Others worked in the field chopping down trees, clearing the land and planting vegetables. The Indians had shown them how to plant corn. Jamestown was a busy place in 1607. It was the beginning of the first permanent English settlement in America.

When summer came, Captain Newport, who was in command of the three ships, left Jamestown for England with the Godspeed and the Susan Constant. He went to bring back food and other things that the colonists needed. Not long after the Captain left, many of the colonists became ill with fever. There were few doctors, no nurses, little medicine, and few knew how to treat the disease. Most of the men were too ill to work, to hunt or to fish, so the food supply nearly ran out. Before winter came nearly one-half of the hundred men had died. The others became discouraged and wanted to return to England. The settling of Virginia was not now a happy time, but always there are stout, brave men.

Among the brave men was Captain John Smith. He was tough and fearless. He was not afraid of Indians, disease, or hunger. Smith was a bold young man who had traveled in Europe and Asia, and fought in battles in Hungary. When winter came with its cold and snow, Captain John Smith went out into the forests to get food from the unfriendly Indians. The Indians captured him and took him to their chief, Wahunsonacock, the Powhatan or great chief of a number of tribes in eastern Virginia. Chief Powhatan and his warriors were angry with the white men. As Smith stood before the Indian chief, the Indians danced and sang songs. John Smith thought that they were going to kill him.

Perhaps the Indians were going to kill Smith. Perhaps the Powhatan wanted to make Smith believe that, and then planned to spare the Englishman's life, adopting Smith into the tribe. In this way, Smith would be forever grateful, and would be willing to give Powhatan gifts such as guns and metal trinkets. However, to Smith, it looked as though he would be killed. The Indians dragged him forward and placed his head on two stones. They stood around him with raised clubs. Then the Powhatan's daughter, Pocahontas, rushed up and put his head in her arms and begged her father to spare his life. No one knows whether this was prearranged. But Smith's life was saved. When he arrived back at Jamestown, he found that there was less food than before and the men were cold and homesick.

Even though Captain Smith was a brave man, he couldn't do everything to keep all of the men and boys from going hungry and cold. He hunted birds and animals for food and tried to keep every one cheerful. But one cold winter day when the men at Jamestown really needed food, they saw Pocahontas with other Indians come out of the forest to the fort and they were carrying baskets of corn and deer meat. Everybody was happy and all started eating. Several times Pocahontas came back bringing more food and soon the white men and Indians were friends again.

Late in the winter Captain Newport returned to Jamestown in the Susan Constant. As the beautiful sailing ship came up the James River, the men and boys on the shore shouted with joy. Some were so happy they cried. Captain Smith was glad, too, because the boat was loaded with food and more than a hundred new colonists landed to make Jamestown their new home. It was a happy time for all in the little Virginia settlement.

The next year, Captain Smith was made the President at Jamestown. He was a hard worker himself and he made every one else work. He knew that every man had to work so that enough vegetables could be raised to keep the colony from starving. Captain Smith told the colonists that if a man didn't work he couldn't eat. He also would not let them say bad words. If a man cursed he had cold water poured down his sleeve. So Captain Smith punished bad men.

Captain Smith learned how to deal with the Indians. He was not afraid of anyone. He soon learned that the Indians liked coins and beads and trinkets. Often he met them in the woods and outside of the fort to trade the things they liked for the food that his colonists needed. It was his duty as head of Jamestown to get food. This helped in keeping the men and women and boys from starving.

Jamestown grew under the leadership of Captain Smith. The fort had been rebuilt into a strong place. There were houses, horses, hogs, sheep, goats, a lot of guns, and many other things that people need. Men went out in boats and fished in the river. Captain Smith had kept the Indians friendly. One of the largest buildings in the settlement was the church. Every Sunday the good people of Jamestown attended services in this little church. Soon Captain Smith had to leave the colony on a trip to England.

JAMESTOWN

Soon after Captain Smith left, the Indians became more hostile. They no longer feared the white men, or provided food for them. The Indians killed the settlers' hogs and stole their guns. They hid outside the fort and ambushed any Englishmen who ventured outside. That winter was known as the Starving Time. Many people died from lack of food, or were killed by the Indians. In the spring, the settlers decided to abandon Jamestown, and go back to England.

Just when all of the colonists were leaving Jamestown to return to England they met Lord Delaware who was coming up the river with three ships, many men and lots of food. He ordered them to go back to Jamestown. They did, and soon under Delaware, the colony took on new life. He had the men rebuild the houses, the landing dock, and the small boats, and work the gardens. He had the church bell ring twice every day to call the people to worship. In a few months Jamestown was a better place in which to work and live. Jamestown was never again to be deserted.

Pocahontas never came to Jamestown after Captain Smith left, but one day some of the white men captured the Indian princess. They took her to the fort and held her a prisoner. She learned to speak English and to wear dresses like the white women. She became a Christian and attended church. In the colony was a young man named John Rolfe. He and Pocahontas fell in love and soon were married in the little church at Jamestown. Many of the Indians from Chief Powhatan's tribe came to see the wedding, so once again Pocahontas brought friendship between the Indians and the settlers.

One of the many things the English at Jamestown learned from the Indians was the use of tobacco. The Indians used it for ceremonies and for smoking. The English had learned about tobacco from Spanish travelers who brought it back from South America. And the English had just started planting tobacco a few years earlier in England. But they saw a lot of tobacco planted in Virginia. However, they thought that Virginia tobacco was too bitter to smoke. John Rolfe, Pocahontas' husband, began to experiment with tobacco from South America. The Englishmen liked it better than the Indians' tobacco.

Tobacco became so popular and so valuable that every family at Jamestown began growing it. Ships came over from England for it. They brought food, clothes and all kinds of needed things to trade for tobacco. On farms all along the James River men were planting tobacco. Many were getting rich by selling it in England. Hundreds of Englishmen came over in ships to Virginia to plant, buy and sell tobacco. Tobacco was now bringing wealth to the colonists. So Jamestown grew and became the Capital of Virginia, and the first permanent English settlement in America.

Many important things happened at Jamestown after the Englishmen began making a lot of money with tobacco. In 1619, the first representative assembly was formed to meet with the Governor, and to pass the first laws made by Englishmen in America. Also in 1619, a Dutch ship brought the first Negro servants to Virginia, and a ship full of young women landed at the dock to marry the bachelors who paid for their passage. A beautiful brick church was built. Horse racing became a popular sport. The Indians, who still were angry that the Englishmen were in Virginia, attacked the settlers in 1622 and 1644, killing large numbers. Jamestown burned four times in the 1600s. Later, in 1699, the Capitol was moved from Jamestown to Middle Plantation, which is now Williamsburg, Virginia. In time, the peninsula became a little island and what was once a bustling, thriving capital in a new land was nearly forgotten, except that today it is one of the greatest shrines in America in a land of Freedom—a place to which every boy and girl should come and see and hear the Past whisper courage to them for the Future.

In 1893, Jamestown was saved for all boys and girls and mothers and fathers by the Association for the Preservation of Virginia Antiquities. This Association of noble women and a few men determined to preserve what was left of Jamestown. It did wonderful work on the old church tower, in building a seawall, in finding old locations, and making the island a beautiful place to visit. Jamestown is now taken care of by this fine Association and the National Park Service.